The Let's Talk Library™

Let's Talk About
Head Lice

Melanie Apel Gordon

The Rosen Publishing Group's
PowerKids Press™
New York

For Carolyn (my teacher), Molly (my co-conspirator), and in memory of Amy (my original inspiration).

Published in 1999 by The Rosen Publishing Group, Inc.
29 East 21st Street, New York, NY 10010

First Edition

Book Design: Erin McKenna

Photo Credits: p. 4 © Telegraph Colour Library/FPG International, p. 7 © 1991 National Medical Slide/Custom Medical Stock, p. 8 © Phyllis Picardi/International Stock, p. 11 © Dusty Wilson/International Stock, p. 12 © Jeffry Myers/FPG International, p. 19 © Montes De Oca, Art/FPG International, p. 20 © Jose Luis Banus.

Photo Illustrations: Cover and pp. 15, 16 by Seth Dinnerman.

Gordon, Melanie Apel.
    Let's talk about head lice / by Melanie Apel Gordon.
        p.   cm. — (Let's talk library)
    Includes index.
    Summary: Discusses infestation with head lice, how it happens, how to treat it, and how to prevent it.
    ISBN 0-8239-5200-2
    1. Pediculosis—Juvenile literature. [1. Pediculosis. 2. Lice] I. Title. II. Series
RL764.P4G67 1998
616.5'7—dc21   97-46758
                                                                          CIP
                                                                          AC

Manufactured in the United States of America

Table of Contents

1 Do I Have Cooties?   5
2 One Louse, Two Lice   6
3 Nits   9
4 Who Gets Lice?   10
5 How Did I Get Lice?   13
6 Lice, Lice Everywhere!   14
7 Lice Be Gone!   17
8 Housecleaning   18
9 Little Bugs on the Little Stuff   21
10 One More Time!   22
    Glossary   23
    Index   24

Ll Mm Nn Oo Pp Qq Rr Ss Tt Uu Vv
ALABAMA
GEORGIA
FLORIDA
ATLANTIC
of Mexico

Do I Have Cooties?

A few kids in Ms. Newton's class are absent today. The teacher said that they have **head lice** (HED LYS). Adam looks around the classroom. Who is missing? He doesn't see Lizzy, Roy, or Stephanie. He thinks they must be the kids who have lice. Before recess the school nurse checks everyone's head for lice. Adam's head feels itchy. The nurse looks through his hair and finds lice. Adam and his head lice have to go home.

◀ Has anyone in your class ever had head lice? Have you?

One Louse, Two Lice

Lice are bugs that live on people's heads. Lice are hard to see because they're tiny. In fact, they are only as big as the dot on the letter *i* in the word *lice*. But if you have lice, you'll know it. Your head will itch! Lice attach themselves to your hair. They bite tiny holes in your **scalp** (SKALP) and suck out little bits of blood. That's what makes your head itch. Lice can only live on heads. But they can lay their eggs anywhere your head has been.

This is what a louse looks like. ▶

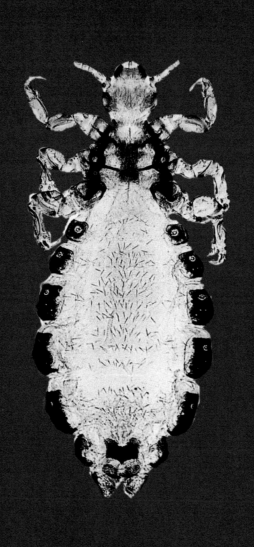

Nits

Lice eggs are called **nits** (NITS). They are easier to see than lice because they are bigger. Nits are yellowish or grayish white and about the size of a sesame seed. Nits stick to your hair. You can't wash nits out of your hair. And you can't blow them out with a hair dryer either. Nits have to be picked out carefully or combed out with a special comb that you can get at the drugstore. If you miss even one nit, the lice can come back.

◀ If your head itches or if someone you know has lice, have a parent or the school nurse check your head carefully.

Who Gets Lice?

More than seven million kids between the ages of five and twelve get lice every year. More kids get lice than all other **contagious** (kun-TAY-jis) sicknesses, except for colds. Anyone can get lice, even grown-ups. Having lice has nothing to do with being clean or dirty. People with clean hair, dirty hair, long hair, and short hair can all get lice. It only takes one louse to **infest** (in-FEST) a head, because that one louse can lay up to ten eggs every day.

Anybody can get lice, but kids get it most often. ▶

Ee Ff Gg Hh Ii Jj Kk Ll Mm Nn Oo Pp Qq Rr Ss Tt

How Did I Get Lice?

Lice can't fly or jump. Instead, they have to be carried from head to head. So they usually catch a ride on things like baseball caps, hats, combs and brushes, coat collars, barrettes, and bows. Kids should never share these things. You shouldn't try on hats in a store either. Most kids get lice from other kids at school. If you get lice, you should stay home from school until you are sure that you have gotten rid of them.

◄ Lice often spread through a classroom by crawling from one jacket to the next in a coat closet.

Lice, Lice Everywhere!

If you get head lice, your head is going to itch a lot. Try not to scratch because you could get an **infection** (in-FEK-shun). Don't be embarrassed if you get head lice. Lots of schools have lice **infestations** (in-fes-TAY-shunz) every year. Most people you know have had lice. Or they know someone else who has had lice. Lice look for warm heads and they don't care who those heads belong to, where those heads live, or how clean or dirty those heads are.

Even if your head itches a lot, try not to scratch too much. You could hurt your scalp. ▶

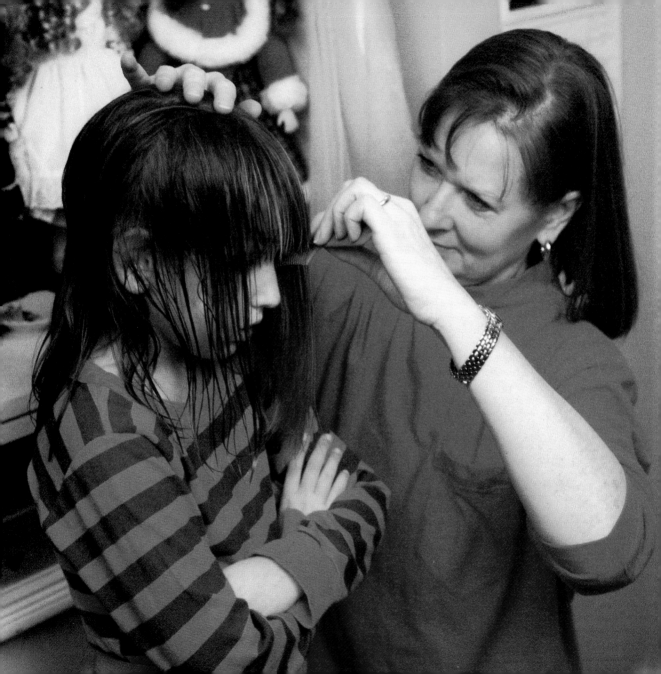

Lice Be Gone!

Water does not kill lice. So trying to wash them out of your hair with regular shampoo won't work. You'll need something stronger. Special shampoo with **pesticides** (PES-tuh-sydz) is made for killing lice. You can buy this shampoo at the drugstore. Have a grown-up read the directions very carefully. Pesticides can be very dangerous. You should wash your hair in the sink so the pesticide shampoo does not get all over your body.

◀ Have your mom or dad help you comb your hair with a special fine-toothed comb after washing with lice-killing shampoo.

Housecleaning

After everyone at home has been **deloused** (dee-LOWST), it's time to clean the house. Carpets, mattresses, sofas, chairs, and any other furniture that your head might have been near should be vacuumed. The vacuum-cleaner bag should be thrown away. Bedsheets, pillowcases, towels, and clothes should be washed in hot water and dried in a hot dryer. Make sure everything is cleaned. You do not have to vacuum your dog or cat. They don't carry lice.

Make sure everything is vacuumed. You don't want the lice to come back. ▶

Little Bugs on the Little Stuff

To make sure that you don't have another lice infestation, everything that's been near your head must also be deloused. Brushes, combs, and barrettes should be boiled in water. Toys that are hard to wash, such as stuffed animals, should be put into plastic bags. Tie the bags shut and put them away for two weeks. Two weeks is enough time for the nits to hatch and die. After two weeks, open the bags outside and shake out the stuffed animals.

◀ Be sure to keep your lice-killing shampoo separate from your regular shampoos.

One More Time!

If you've had lice once, you won't want lice twice. Important things to remember are:

- Don't share caps, hats, or coats.
- Don't share combs and brushes.
- If someone you know has lice and your head starts to itch, get checked for lice.
- Get rid of lice quickly.

And most important, don't be embarrassed if you get head lice. Lice have been around for millions of years. You're not the only kid who's ever had them.

Glossary

contagious (kun-TAY-jis) When a sickness can be passed from one person to another.

delouse (dee-LOWS) To get rid of lice.

head lice (HED LYS) Small insects that live on people's heads.

infection (in-FEK-shun) A disease caused by germs.

infest (in-FEST) To take over something.

infestation (in-fes-TAY-shun) When something is overrun by a large number of something dangerous or unhealthy (like head lice).

nits (NITS) Lice eggs.

pesticide (PES-tuh-syd) A chemical that kills bugs.

scalp (SKALP) The skin on your head under your hair.

Index

B
barrettes, 13, 21
baseball caps, 13, 22
bows, for hair, 13
brushes and combs, 13, 21, 22

C
cases, number of, 10
checking, for head lice, 5, 22
coats, 13, 22
contagious, 10

D
delouse, 18, 21

drugstore, 17

H
hats, 13, 22

I
infection, 14
infest, 10
infestation, 14
itchiness, 5, 6, 14, 22

L
lice, how they travel, 13
lice eggs, 6, 9, 10

N
nits, 9, 21

P
pesticide, 17

S
scalp, 6
school nurse, 5
shampoo, to kill lice, 17
size, of lice, 6

T
toys, 21